MW00790709

A Collection of Smart Comments for Report Cards

Nevelon T. Gaitor

A Collection of
Smart
Comments
for Report Cards

ISBN: 978-0-9847460-6-4

Design and Layout by Mr. Michael J. Matulka of Basik Studios
Omaha, Nebraska USA

Published by Basik Studios (*www.gobasik.com*)
Omaha, Nebraska USA

Printed in the USA

Resource Information:

The writer's research on the subject and general interest, credited those experienced educators who are well acquainted with today's classroom management and evaluative skills. For further research, you would find books that address curriculum based topics and provided creative suggestions on crafting your smart comments.

- Early Childhood Education

- Behavior, Discipline , and Guidance

- Learning Disabilities in Children

- Positive Attitude and Self-Esteem

- Professional Development and Management Skills

- Numeracy and Literacy Skills

- Fearon Teacher - Aid Books - Mavie McDonald

- Positive Behavior Intervention and Support

Climb Every Mountain

Follow Every Rainbow

Till You Find Your Dream....

- Oscar Hammerstein II

Acknowledgements

Thanks to Almighty God for the wisdom, knowledge and inspiration to produce, in written form, some suggestions that have been considered, "smart comments for students report card".

To my wife Olive, who pushes me out of my comfort zone and provided the kind of support that allowed me to persevere in spite of many challenges and distractions. Thank you!

I express gratitude to the many colleagues whose encouragements gave me a positive direction that allowed me to follow my dream. Your involvement helped me to transform the interpretation of comments for report card into a catalogue that can be useful to teachers.

Sincere appreciation to my parents, Ishmael and Beatrice Gaitor, (*deceased*), the patriarch and matriarch of the family. They have been the nuclei in shaping my destiny.

To all teachers, you worked well, and your commitment to service pays off in the lives of your students. That is why you deserve a smile today and every day. Honorable mention to Mrs. Kiffany Daxon, Rujean Hart and Rev. Neil Hamilton JP, for their encouragement and assistance. Thank you also to the Teacher of the Year at S.C. McPherson Jr. High School 2014-2016, Ms. Bennique I. Brown for willingly consenting to edit these smart comments. May God Bless ALL of you!

About the Writer

Nevelon Theophilus Gaitor is a certified-professional high school teacher, a veteran educator, experienced Vice Principal in the Public School system. He has served in the capacity as Vice Principal Administration and Curriculum at the Junior and Senior High levels in New Providence, Bahamas.

He has successfully completed the Educational Management certification course sponsored by The Department of Education. He holds undergraduate degrees from The College of The Bahamas, The University of The West Indies Board of Education and Saint Benedict College & Saint John's University Collegeville, Minnesota, U.S.A. Mr. Gaitor resides with his wife, Olive, and children, Kenya Gaitor-Ferguson and Kerim Ormond Jason Gaitor in Nassau, Bahamas.

His spiritual foundation is built on biblical principles and the belief that he can do all things through Christ who strengthens him. He has a passion for education, a vision for the future and the commitment to ensure that all students maximize their potential. His hobbies include reading, music, farming and carpentry. He is a native son of Cat Island and is proud to be a Bahamian.

Nevelon T. Gaitor, *Educator*
P. O. Box CB 12620
Nassau, Bahamas
gaitorman@hotmail.com

Preface

According to Meg McDelgan, "Report Cards help to summarize the student's progress for both the student and parent." It is important to note that parents and guardians view the teacher's message as a mirror of truth in progress.

Partnership with parents can create an atmosphere of trust by maintaining proper working relationship between the home and school. As a result of written comments, many parents form their opinion about the school's academic programs and the kind of learning environment that exist at school. Thus, it is important that the comments begin with a positive approach and be tactfully stated, concise, and grammatically correct.

Smart comments for Report Card contain suggestions and examples that covers a wide range of classroom and practical situations. Each area is design specifically to deal with a common problem, and the messages are categorized for that purpose. Weak work; behavior, personality, poor attendance and tardiness; average, slow, bright, a new student, the inclusive child and end-of-term messages are some of the sub topics. In addition, as a guide, the Appendix contains a list of adjectives that are particularly useful for teacher's comments. There is also a list of suggested phrases that is significant to the situation and consistent with the student's behavior pattern and ability to perform at a reasonable standard.

Perhaps, smart comments would be the agent of change that allow teachers to appreciate the option not only to work harder but to work smarter. The suggestions and examples would be a model for new teachers to follow as they focus on each child's progress and ability to learn. However, it is essential that each comment reflects the specific need of the child so that the parent or guardian would appreciate its' importance. The comments are intended to create a partnership with parents and to ensure that they understand the individual differences of each child as he or she develop holistically.

As I reflect upon the primary reason for writing a collection of smart comments, I am most appreciative of the opportunity to read and approve thousands of positive comments attributed to students by their teachers. Commendable!

Contents

Chapter 1
Weak, Slow, and Unproductive Work

Numeracy

_____ has a good attitude towards the work at this grade level. It would help his speed in arithmetic if more time is spent each evening on multiplication facts. He is a shy child and it would help him more if he can practice mixed operations and number patterns.

_____ is a helpful student and she enjoys our devotions. I feel that a conference with you would be beneficial at this time, because we would discuss her progress and determine if we could give her more guidance in arithmetic.

_____ has a good attitude towards group work. As this report shows, he is having a great deal of trouble with arithmetic. However, he needs to study every evening, starting with two-column addition and subtraction. Could you help him with these problems in a quiet environment?

_____ is a fine student and she is anxious to participate and complete the assignment. Her progress in arithmetic is not consistent. However, she still needs to review, on a consistent basis, multiplication facts and addition of whole numbers.

_____ has shown improvement in her relationships with others. She needs our encouragement frequently. She lacks the basics to master the concepts and skills at the foundation level in arithmetic. Perhaps a conference would enable us to seek additional help for her.

Thank you for your interest in providing the multiplication poster board for the classroom. It would be helpful if you can provide a similar chart for the home environment. _____ will appreciate the effort as a reward.

Thank you for your cooperation with _____'s mathematics project. However, as stated in the report, _____'s conduct is affecting his work academically. I would suggest that you remind him about his general conduct and focus on improving his grades in arithmetic.

_____'s vocabulary has improved. It is evident that you are helping her at home. However, she is still having problems with arithmetic concepts. There seems to be no consistency with her overall arithmetic skills. I think it would be appropriate to discuss new strategies by phone rather than having another conference.

Comprehension Skills
Language Arts

_____ 's difficulty in writing seems to be largely a problem of muscular coordination. He will have to make a consistent effort to improve his penmanship over a period of time.

_____ speaks very well in dialogue with his peers. However, he does need to improve his written language. With greater effort and more careful practice, there should be progress.

Thank you for your visit during open house. _____ was very happy with your visit. Reading library books may improve his vocabulary. Ensure that he studies the spelling list every night and find the appropriate meaning of new words.

_____ has shown an increased interest in the study of current events and cartoons. It will be helpful if she practice the list of spelling words at home.

Chapter 2
Behavior Problems

Respect

_____ is trying hard to practice good habits. Realizing that conforming to the rules meant respecting others is the first step in the right direction. He needs to use problem solving skills to resolve conflicts consistently.

_____ does the best she can in the basic skills area. However, she should avoid acting in such a manner as to expose others to risk or danger.

_____ experienced great difficulty in adjusting to the new school environ- ment. However, he is again trying very hard to respect the rights and property of others. Encourage him to accept responsibility for his behavior.

_____ is becoming one of the most disrespectful students in the class. She has not taken responsibility for her actions. Occasionally, she had been referred for counseling for unacceptable behavior.

Work Habits

Thank you for attending the conference. _____ has made some progress in his personality problems, but he still needs a great deal of guidance and supervision in order to work well. I suggest you set aside a time each evening when both of you can communicate and identify important issues.

_____ seems to have difficulty settling down in class. He tends to be quite impatient and gets upset easily. However, with his enthusiasm and sincerity, I am certain he will develop greater stability. I appreciate the patience and understanding you have demonstrated.

_____ has been progressing nicely. His greatest problem has been his inability to listen attentively and keep his mind focus. He is inclined to draw attention repeatedly to distract his peers from important instructions.

_____ is doing good work in the basic skills area. However she is not showing the desired growth in social maturity. She is often out of her seat wanting attention about trivial matters. She pouts frequently if she is reprimanded for her actions. I would like a conference with you immediately.

Attitude

Although there has been some improvement in _____'s attitude towards school, he is not consistent with his class assignments. Therefore, he will need guidance and encouragement to improve his attitude.

_____'s report card is a reflection of his attitude in school. He could do bet- ter if he decides to work and cooperate.

Thank you for our recent conference. As we discussed _____'s attitude and work ethics, she needs to realize and appreciate the opportunity available and apply herself fully to obtain better results.

_____'s attitude, and social involvement are inconsistent. He requires much supervision because he is far too interested in his peers than academics. Encourage him to focus on areas of weaknesses in reading.

_____'s attitude toward school rules need to be improved considerably. He is very defiant to his teachers and the support staff.

Relations with Peers

_____'s progress in her school work is not as strong as it was the first term. This is because she continues to have difficulties in her relationship with other students and conforming to school rules. This affects her grades and is evident on the progress report.

I am very pleased with _____'s class work. His writing is especially neat. However, he is having considerable difficulty in his relationships with his peers, which is causing much unhappiness. I feel it is important that we have a conference soon.

General

Thank you for your conference with the principal about _____'s behavior. It is hoped that he conform to the rules of the school.

_____ certainly enjoys arithmetic and continues to do outstanding work in his class. Encourage him for his effort.

_____ is a serious student and tries hard to succeed. He has the ability to do excellent work but is prevented by tenseness. He is very excited and needs to be taught to relax.

I would like to have a conference with you soon concerning _____'s behav- ior. He has trouble keeping his hands to himself and this creates frequent disturbances. It is necessary to remind him frequently that at school, we must cooperate with others.

_____ has settled down and is beginning to do better work. I hope that his renewed interest in school and improvement in his behavior will continue.

Chapter 3
Recreational Behavior

_____ really does some impressive work in Art & Craft. He certainly uses his imagination extremely well and it is commendable. However, he sometimes feel intimidated because of his size during playground activities. Would you come and discuss this matter with me please?

_____'s class-work is frequently affected by difficulties that started on the playground. He must remember that there are rules for physical activities and it would help if he practice teamwork. Encourage him to socialize more with others.

_____ is a fine athlete and has the potential of a good leader. However, because of his poor sportsmanship, he is involved in too many arguments. It may become necessary to remove him from the extra-curricula activities for a short period of time. You are asked to report to school for a conference immediately.

_____ works hard on her assignments. Sometimes negative comments from her peers cause her unhappiness, and this is reflected in group work activities. She is not showing the desired growth in maturity for this grade level.

_____ is a humorous child, but she needs to follow instructions and contribute to the success of the team. She has good organizational skills that can be helpful to others.

_____ is a very good student. His interest in _____ is stimulating to the class. It would help him if he participates in a variety of playground games.

Chapter 4
Personality Problems

Self-Confidence

_____ has gained much self-confidence. This has given him the feeling of success in his work. He is easy to get along with and expects no special privileges.

_____ is showing great improvement in Modern Languages and she is excited. She leads the discussions in class and is consistently gaining self-confidence.

Thank you for viewing the class display. There is a need for _____ to take part in classroom discussions and develop more confidence in himself. Please encourage him more.

_____ is inclined to be timid and shy. More practice in oral reading may develop self-confidence.

_____ is a conscientious student and a responsible member of the school band. It would help him gain more confidence in himself if he observes and participates in performing arts productions.

_____ is overanxious and worries about his work at times, which is probably a lack of self-confidence. He requires a great deal of praise and attention. Encourage him to develop good study habits and relax.

_____ needs more confidence in herself before she can do good work. She is inclined to be dependent upon others for directions. Encourage her to follow simple instructions.

Shyness

Thank you for your telephone calls. _____ still has trouble expressing himself orally because of his shyness. However, I have noticed a little improvement the past few weeks.

_____ has made some adjustment this term at school. She is a shy student, but I am confident that being elected class captain will help her in this area. She is very honest and dependable.

_____ is now reading at grade three level. He is beginning to contribute to the conversations and discussions in class and seems to be overcoming his shyness.

Chapter 5
IMPROVEMENT AND GROWTH

Social

I appreciate your timely visit to our class. I am happy to report that _____ is showing growth in her social relations with other students. She seems to be happier and more at ease in the school environment.

I certainly appreciate your cooperation with _____ this term. She has worked very hard, and although she is not perfect in her social maturity, it is a problem that can be solved under your guidance.

_____ has made progress this term, especially making the necessary adjust- ment socially. Thank you for your cooperation.

_____ has made fine progress in most of the practical subjects this term. Please continue to commend him for the growth he has made socially and academically.

_____ will continue to need your guidance in overcoming his personality problems. He will find school much more pleasant if he is able to sustain the improvement he has shown this term.

Thank you for the commitment you have shown this term to assist _____ with the information for his coursework. It is obvious that you are involve in your child's education.

Attitude

_____'s attitude is much better now, and he is learning more self-control. Encouragement is necessary for him to build self-esteem. However, he is to be commended for his skills in physical education activities.

I am very pleased with _____'s improvement after our conference. She knows that we care about her success. You deserve the credit for the positive approach that you have taken to help foster good attitude.

Thank you for the confidence you have in _____. I am delighted with the improvement that he has made with his behavior problems. It is evident that he is dependable, and his work ethics reflects the new attitude

_____ is improving consistently in her overall attitude and should be encourage to do enrichment activities in class. I am happy to discuss her progress with you.

_____ has shown improvement in many areas of school work. Now she is ambitious and maturing nicely, please encourage her to continue this trend. She has a pleasant disposition and is most cooperative.

General

Thank you for your interest and cooperation. It is evident that _____ is studying at home. There has been improvement in her arithmetic and reading skills. Please encourage her to improve in the area of creative writing.

For several weeks, _____ showed improvement in problem solving. However, his written work is not up to standard. Therefore, I feel that an immediate conference with you would be most helpful.

_____ has improved since our last conference, but he needs to practice con- structing short sentences and paragraphs for the next assignment. I would kindly recommend additional help.

_____ shows great enthusiasm in school work. He enjoys reading and poetry. However, it would help his physical and mental abilities if he participates in sports.

_____ is very good at creative arts. It is evident in his painting of still-life and portraits that he is talented. Encourage him to maximize his potential.

_____ follow instructions very well. He is talented and willing to assist his peers if necessary. He must be commended for his honesty and positive attitude.

Chapter 6
Poor Attendance and Tardiness

Absences

_____ does very good work when he attends school, but his frequent absences is the primary reason for most of his below average grades. Could you encourage him to attend school often.?

_____ has had difficulty adjusting to the work schedule. His frequent absences are reflected in the quality of class work he has produced. You are invited to discuss the his attendance at a conference immediately.

It is difficult to make an accurate evaluation of _____'s progress at this time because of her frequent absences. Together we can encourage her to be consistent in school attendance.

_____'s frequent absences make it difficult for her to keep up with her classmates. She sometimes complain about not feeling well in class but displayed the opposite during playground activities.

Tardiness

_____ is tardiness is unacceptable. He needs to arrive early for class and completes home work assignments as required. Encourage him to make the effort to improve his time management skills.

At the beginning of the term there were improvement in _____'s attitude and punctuality. However, she frequently arrives late and her tardiness disrupts the class.

Chapter 7
The Average Child

Academic Performance

_____ is a dependable and very cooperative in class. He takes active part in all of the activities. His oral reading is fluent and his comprehension skills have improved significantly. He takes pride in his work and his presentation is neat.

_____ has done well in assuming her prefect duties but is an average student. She is having difficulty adjusting to the new school environment. I am confident that she will cope with the changes soon.

Encourage _____ to read more books and practice finding the meaning of new words. By doing so, it would improve his vocabulary and comprehension skills.

_____ takes keen interest in all assignments and completes them well. During the term, she has contributed useful information and materials to the class science project. I really enjoyed working with her and it has been a pleasure having her as my student.

_____ shows satisfactory progress in his work. Thank you for helping to motivate and stimulate his interest. However, he tends to work too rapidly, which often results in careless mistakes. Encourage him to take his time.

_____ volunteers often. She has develop the speed necessary to compete in her keyboarding class. However, she needs to complete home work assignments and turn them in on time.

Attitude

_____'s attitude towards school is excellent. He takes great pride in per- forming at a high standard and representing the school well.

_____ is a cooperative and mannerly student who accepts responsibility for his actions. You can always depend on him to set good example for others to follow. It is a pleasure having him in my class. He is a role model.

Thank you for the fine characteristics _____ have developed over the years. Certainly you have done an excellent job in molding a fine Bahamian citizen.

General

_____ is doing very well and has made rapid progress to move to the next level grade level. Encourage her to continue this trend in the future.

_____ is a very enthusiastic member of the basketball team. He takes on the responsibility as the leader and provide the kind of leadership which is necessary to win. We commend him for his outstanding efforts.

As a result of self-esteem, _____ has acquired poise and self-confidence and now she appears ready to perform without hesitancy. This improvement is due in part to her realization that she is rapidly mastering the fundamental skills necessary to succeed.

In his tranquil way, _____ is very helpful in class. His generosity and friendly gesture always help to put his peers at ease. I am proud to have him as a student of my class.

Chapter 8
The Bright Child

Academic Performance

_____ has produced excellent work this term. He has consistently achieved a high standard over the years and enjoys reading as a hobby.

_____'s excellent work is a reflection of his fine attitude and outstanding effort. The entire class has enjoyed the many interesting articles that he has brought to share with other students during our silent reading time.

You can be very proud of _____ because she is mannerly and respectful. It has been a pleasure to work with such a conscientious individual.

_____ is a cooperative and affectionate student. He is very serious about his involvement in class competitions and has accomplished much academically.

_____ is an outstanding student who completes her work accurately. She always find desirable ways to occupy her extra time. It is a pleasure to work with such a student who is focused and determined to achieve.

With _____'s ability to apply himself academically, he will receive excel- lent results on his progress report card.

Presently _____ has developed good potential. If she will persevere and continue to work hard in the future, she will benefit a great deal from the educational experiences.

Chapter 9
The Slow Student

Academic Performance

_____ is a pleasant student. She is always polite and cooperative in class. Although she is making steady progress in her school work, she has not mastered the required skills to move to the next grade level. I am concerned as to whether her achievement will be sufficient for her to be promoted to the next grade.

I am extremely pleased with the way _____ has learned to follow directions and complete assignments independently. He seems to enjoy working with in small groups. However, he has been rather slow in acquiring the necessary skills for the next grade level.

Thank you for attending the conference. As we discussed, _____'s work is below the normal standards. She needs to learn to concentrate and improve her study habits.

It is a pleasure working with _____ this year. He has shown growth in reading, and writing, but he is not ready for success at the next level. Perhaps it would be prudent if he spends another year strengthening his academic foundation.

I am concerned about _____'s progress at the present grade level. The overall picture is not good. His work habits and social growth have not improve satisfactorily. slow improvement. Please attend the next parent /teacher conference.

Attitude

_____ tries his very best , but there are some concern s with his personal problems. He lacks self-confidence and become very nervous when asked to read aloud. Please encourage him to have more confidence in order to progress.

_____ does average grade-level work. However, I am certain he is capable of doing better if he concentrates more on his studies. He tends to be more interested in friendship rather than completing class work.

Although there has been slow improvement in _____'s attitude in class, it is not consistent with the response and behavior at sporting events.

_____ is slow in responding to the safety rules in the workshop. He must consider safety an important part of the instructional process. It would take a combined effort to help him improve his attitude.

As my reports have indicated, _____ is not doing well on his homework assignments. She seems not to care about the correctness of information and presentation of work. If this continues, she will not be allowed to enjoy the fun day activities.

_____ realizes the importance of a positive attitude. Thank you for the role you have played in helping him to acknowledge his conduct.

Chapter 10
The New Student

Adjustment

_____ has been in my class for a short period of time, and it is difficult to evaluate his personality. However, I can see that he has found it difficult to adjust to the new classroom environment. I would be most appreciative if you can attend a conference.

For a short time, _____ had difficulty adjusting to his new school. How- ever, he has made an effort to overcome this and now settled remarkably well. His work ethics is consistent with his ability to perform at a high standard.

It would be difficult to make an accurate evaluation of _____'s work, since he has not been with us too long. He does have difficulty in her relations with others and this has been affecting his assignments.

_____ has had extreme difficulty in adjusting to his new environment. I would be most appreciative if you attend a conference so that you would become aware of the concern.

It is difficult to give _____ a fair evaluation at this time because it has only been a few weeks since she has join the class. However, she can do well at the end of the reporting period if she is willing to double the effort and work harder.

_____ is an extraordinary student who has made tremendous progress in adjusting to his new school. He is fully involved in the general subject areas and I am very impressed with his overall performance.

Chapter 11
End-of-School Messages

Academic Performance

_____ has matured socially and academically this school year. She assumes responsibility well and has a fine attitude generally. However, it would help if she is consistent in preparation for the final examinations.

There has been a noticeable improvement in _____'s study habits during this term which is encouraging. This shows that hard work and commitment produce good results.

With _____'s ability to apply himself to the task, he should receive an excellent grade for oral reporting and reading. The involvement in the drama club has help him gained confidence and sharpened his comprehension skills.

Attitude

Thank you for your interest in _____'s attitude. Although he has had some difficulty adjusting to the classroom environment, his performance as a prefect is encouraging.

I am proud to report that _____ is progressing very well. She has made positive contributions to our class and is an inspiration to her classmates. With her friendly, and cooperative attitude, she will always be a pleasant student with much humor.

Regardless of how busy _____ is, she is always willing to assist others. For this reason, she is appreciated by the majority of the students in her class. Encourage her to continue to display positive attitude and be the kind of example that others would want to follow.

_____ is a pleasant and conscientious student. He is proud to be the school's head boy, and this responsibility seems to have given him much enthusiasm to serve. You are to be commended for grooming such a gentleman and it has been a pleasure to have him in my class.

_____ enjoys the responsibility of class captain. She ensures that the classroom rules are consistently followed by all students. She is respectful and honest with her peers. However, she needs to strengthen the basic skills in arithmetic and comprehension.

_____ is a student with great potential but he needs to settle down and focus more on his school work. With a positive attitude and self-control, he would be able to make steady progress. Encouragement is highly recommended at this time.

_____ has performed exceptionally well this term. He is a diligent worker and does not require frequent supervision with basic task. Encourage him to utilize the study schedule effectively.

Without a doubt, _____'s attitude has change rapidly and now she is cooperating with other students during playground activities. This is indeed a positive trend.

Chapter 12
The Inclusion Child

Most parents are aware of the challenges and experiences a child with disabilities faced in the society. Information from the child's physician help parents to understand the limitations and the appropriate ability level of the individual. Therefore, teachers should focus on simple comments rather than giving the parents inaccurate impression of the child's performance.

(*Individualized Education Plan*)

General

_____ is working hard and showing eagerness to learn new skills.

_____ is strengthening her skills in matching shapes and colors.

_____ has a good personality, kind to others and makes friends easily.

_____ is learning to listen carefully to instructions before responding.

_____ is learning to share with others and participate in playground activities.

_____'s attitude towards attending school is positive and she is an eager classroom helper.

_____ is identifying new words at the appropriate level. He shows interest in story books.

APPENDIX 1

It is possible at times to convey an accurate evaluation of a student by using short phrase. Although many of them can be used appropriately in a variety of situations, the teacher can choose the comments that are suitable and meaningful for the individual report.

- Needs to practice oral speaking more distinctly.

- Does not complete class assignments in the allotted time.

- Sacrificing accuracy for unnecessary speed in her written work.

- Fails to complete individual assignments.

- Comprehends well, but work very slow.

- Would improve if she develops a greater interest in arithmetic.

- Needs to strengthen skills in comprehension.

- Language handicap is main source of difficulty.

- Not working to full capability.

- Lack of interest in work.

- Has ability but not applying himself.

- Is doing the work hastily rather than carefully.

- Is working extremely hard to master _____ and is making progress.

- Needs constant supervision.

- Not too concern about her behavior.

- Needs to improve in self-control so that he will find greater social acceptance.

- Is learning to share and listen.

- Is becoming more dependable during work periods.

- Wants responsibilities, but fails to follow through as a leader.

- Needs to play a more active role in class discussion.

- Has shown improvement in her academics, but more self-control is needed.

- Needs to respect the rights and property of others.

- Respect those in authority and obey all school rules.

- Is learning to be a better listener, which enables him to follow directions more promptly.

- Needs to improve her playground relations with others.

- Is learning to be careful, cooperative, and fair.

- Is continuing to grow socially and independently.

- Is aggressive in the classroom and on playground.

- Never reluctant about participating in extra curricula activities.

- Doesn't volunteer often but is willing to take part in class work when requested.

- Has a pleasant personality and improved steadily.

- Is improving in reading, especially vocabulary development.

- Thank you for stimulating _____ interest in book reports.

- Has improved his numeracy and literacy skills.

- Has shown a good attitude and is gaining self-confidence.

- Has improve in general comprehension skills.

- Works well with peers and is pleased with her fluent oral reading.

- Shows pride in her work.

- Attitude towards school is excellent.

- Has a sense of humor and enjoys the stories we read.

- Is a steadfast, conscientious worker.

- Expresses herself well through art and drama.

- Apply skills to all written assignments.

- Quality of work is improving in social studies and arithmetic.

- Is maintaining grade-level achievements.

- Work well in groups, planning and executing activities.

- Is an enthusiastic worker with great talent and disposition.

- Needs to develop a better sense of responsibility.

- Excels in writing original stories and poems.

- Has good organization of thoughts.

- Has a vast background knowledge of culture.

- Needs to practice more to improve penmanship.

- Cooperative, well-mannered and talented student.

- Good worker and attentive listener.

- Frequently absent from school.

- Parent /teacher conference needed.

- Disrespectful to teachers.

- Must improve study habits.

APPENDIX II

This appendix contains a list of appropriate adjectives to convey an accurate evaluation of a student. Teachers can choose the appropriate adjectives for the comments that will have personal application to a specific student.

Choose the Appropriate Adjectives

Affectionate	Aggressive
Alert	Ambitious
Appreciative	Capable
Conscientious	Consistent
Consistent	Cooperative
Courteous	Defiant
Dependable	Disobedient
Disrespectful	Domineering
Disorderly	Destructive
Eager	Enthusiastic

Friendly	Imaginative
Impolite	Inattentive
Inconsistent	Interested
Overcritical	Poised
Quiet	Reserved
Serious	Talkative
Talented	Well-adjusted

Instructional Engagement

Student's Participation

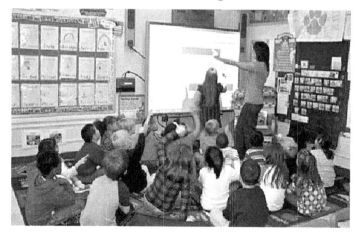

A Reflection of the Past

Capturing the Moment of Anticipation

A Simple Thought
Attributed to Teachers

As a teacher, remember that you should enter the classroom each day with one goal in mind; and that is to empower all students to maximize their potential. However, the most important question you should ask yourself is, what could my students learn, master, perfect, or understand better today than they did yesterday?

Without a doubt, you would have carefully facilitated the kind of learning experiences that would ensure your students equitable access to a rich and meaningful education. Therefore, you should challenge them so that they would excel beyond the normal potential regardless of their behavior, color, creed, origin, disability, strengths or social needs.

The choice is yours. The teaching profession is the most noblest of all professions and your core values of striving for excellence should not prevent you from delivering quality education to all students.

Your primary focus should be to elicit the insight of others, dialogue with stakeholders in the community and consistently provide meaningful learning experiences for your students that would positively impact their lives.

Teachers sometimes become frustrated when faced with difficult challenges. Human nature at times present the most unpredictable circumstances that would change the outcome. You must not give up but persevere because the prize would not be given to those who are swift in action; but those who finish the race. You mus remain true to your core values and beliefs that every student can learn. As you chose the appropriate comments for each child's report, may it be an accurate and a meaningful evaluation.

Let the Children Tell Their Stories

Stories are like a rainbow in the sky with colors that attract adult and children alike. The radiance on the child's face tells the story of the excitement from a glimpse of the rainbow to its' rapid disappearance.

We are obliged to listen, because each child has a story to tell. Yet as the story unfolded, one would better appreciate the reasons fo the child's lack of selfesteem, confidence, attitude and academic performance.

Listen to Matt's story as it is told to an audience of parents, teacher and admin- istrators at a graduation ceremony. Matt is a fictitious name given in the story for the protection of the individual's identity and nationality.

Fourteen years ago, a mother abandoned her child on the city dump. But lucki- ly, an old man found the child and decided tha he would take on the responsibility of caring and educating him A few years later, he reported to the police that the child can no learn and is speedily turning into a dangerous criminal.

The Police listened attentively to the old man's story, investigated the allegation then decided that the child can learn and was not a criminal. Without a doubt, the child's untold experiences made life difficult.

Unfortunately, his rebellious attitude and lack of respect for adults were unac- ceptable. Some time later, the old man died and Matt was left alone to care for himself. He slept in abandoned vehicles as shelter from elements and feed himself with food left in garbage bins in the community.

Let the child's story be told: Matt communicated well with his peers and was determined to make something positive out of life. He rejected the opportunity of hanging out on street corners with friends, but at the same time, embraced the idea of being alone.

School life was depressing as he found it difficult adjusting to the classroom environment at his new school. Some of Matt's teachers were frustrated with his negative behavior and did not understand the circumstances that lead to the behavioral problems. His situations were not normal because of society's constant reminder that he was the child abandoned by his mother on the city dump at an early age.

As the story progressed, Matt was asked to traced his family roots, but he replied, "I am not interested." His desire was that God provide someone who would help him actualize his dream of becoming a pilot. When he would have accomplished his goals with certainty, then he would fly away to a new country where no one knew his past.

In spite of Matt's unfortunate circumstances, there is hope for the depressed, marginalized and underprivileged children. Listen to their stories and offer hope for a better tomorrow.

Now you know that stories are like rainbows. Teachers, you would have encountered many students with similar stories to tell. Do not close your eyes to the rainbow. The child who has been disruptive in your class, lacks respect for authority, displays a negative attitude, lacks self-esteem and confidence, easily distracted, talks excessively, and have a poor attendance at school, has a story to tell. Perhaps, if given a second chance, he could be useful in society.

Every child can learn if given the opportunity and the environment conducive for learning. Smart Comments for Report was written primarily to assist teachers create relevant messages about students.

Listen to My Story

The names of the characters in my story are fictitious in order to protect the identity and nationality of the individuals.

Without a doubt, you would have heard similar stories but I believe Sarah's story is pathetic, powerful and deserve the audience attention.

Sarah was Mrs. Rolle's favorite. She entered Grade 1 reading at Grade 6 Level. Everyone admitted that she was too small to be five years old. She stood at approximately three feet eight inches tall and looked like the wind could pick her up and cause her to sail through the air like a kite. But in the classroom, Sarah was a giant. She was always writing and helping other students.

All of her teachers were very sad when it was time for her to move on to the next grade level. Each of them wishing for another Sarah.

Every report card Sarah received from Grade 1 to 5 had a 4.0 Grade Point Average. It was a pleasure for her parents to collect the Report Cards and listen to the glowing comments from Sarah's teachers.

Sarah's parents did not have a high school diploma but they taught her the value of an education. They made sure that she had all of the materials she needed for every class although that meant less money for her to purchase lunch.

Mrs. Baxter could not wait for Sarah to enter her Grade 6 class. She had heard so many wonderful and interesting things about Sarah that she made a bright yellow Teacher's Assistant Badge and await her arrival. When Sarah was presented with her badge, all of the students envied her. They knew Mrs. Baxter gave the best incentives and even had a Bulletin Board just for the student of the week.

But, something wasn't right.

After the first two weeks, Mrs. Baxter took her badge back from Sarah. She talked about how Sarah spent all of her time in the Nurse's Office complaining about headaches. She even told the Principal that all of Sarah's teachers had inflated her grades because she could barely read. For her, she insisted that the Principal placed Sarah in one of the Special Education classes where she belong or she would ask for an immediate re-assignment.

Faced with that ultimatum, the Principal investigated and decided that Sarah's grades have decreased significantly. She was then placed in a Special Education class. The students laughed at her as she entered the room. Mrs. Samuel, the Resource Teacher silenced them.

Mrs. Samuel on the other hand, told the Principal that there had to be some mistake. She reminded him that she had marked Sarah's entrance examinations papers and listened to her read fluently. She also provided pictures of Sarah accepting the School's Spelling Competition Awards four consecutive years in a row.

As soon as Sarah could catch her breath to speak, she asked to go to the Nurse's Office. Mrs. Samuel asked her, why? She explained that she had a severe headache. Sarah eyes appeared not to be focused as she tried to read the words from the flash cards. Mrs. Samuel was puzzled then she asked Sarah how long she had experienced the headaches. Sarah admitted that the headaches had started several months ago but she did not inform her parents.

Sarah was immediately taken to the Nurse's Office for eye examination. The results from Sara's eye examination showed that she had lost vision in one eye.

Unfortunately, Sarah's lost of vision in one eye came as a surprise to her teachers and parents. Perhaps, with Sarah's frequent visit to the Nurse's Office, could have been an indication for immediate action and preventive measures.

Sarah recovered from the eye surgery was successful and although she had been absent for three months from school, she was prepared to work hard. Without a doubt, Sarah's academic performance at the end of Grade 6 was impressive and she was the choice for student of excellence. Sarah was awarded the top honor for academic excellence and given a Merit Scholarship for outstanding performance at the Primary School level during the Prize Giving Ceremony.

Every child is special and unique as a human being. Even though there are differences and similarities in the child's attitude and behavior. As an adults, it is required of us that we provide the spirit of hope and a commitment to shape the destiny of the child.

Sarah's story has given us a glimpse of the outcome, as a result of hasty decision, without proper examination of the reasons that lead to her inability to read fluently. Perhaps, we can only assume that there are more individuals in our schools with similar stories. But before you form your opinion about Sarah's unfortunate situation, Stop! Think! And Listen to her story!

A Collection of
Smart
Comments
for Report Cards

Nevelon T. Gaitor

Made in the USA
Las Vegas, NV
16 November 2021